DATE DUE

OCT 12		
JAN 16		
MAY 2		
MAY 1997		
OCT 8		
OCT 21		
APR 04		
APR 21 MAY 3		
MAY 13		

The Story of
THE ALAMO

By Norman Richards

Illustrations by Tom Dunnington

ℙ CHILDRENS PRESS, CHICAGO

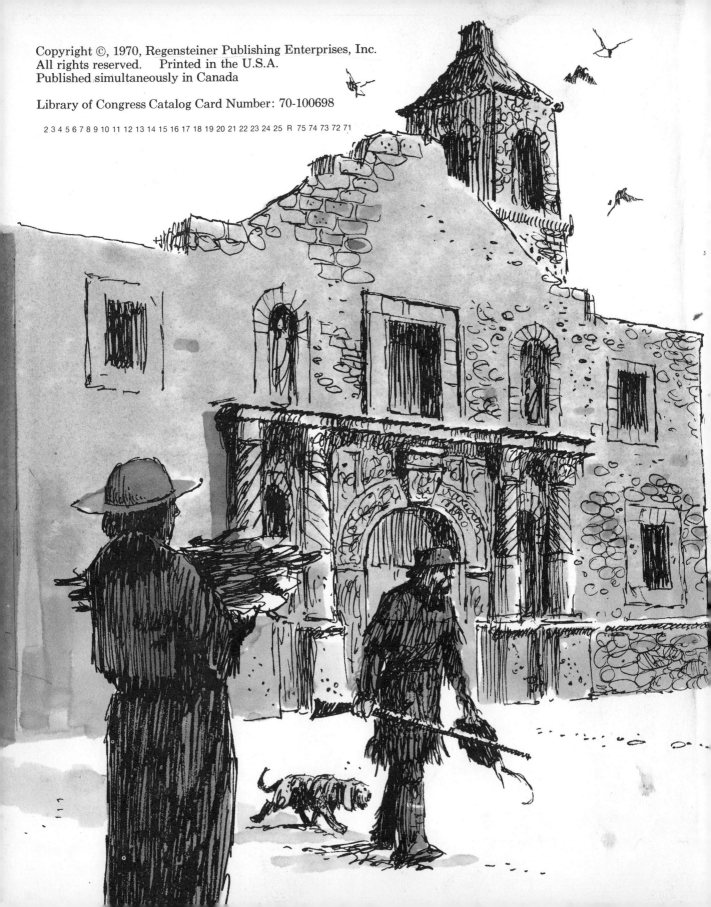

Long ago, when most of the colonies on the Atlantic coast of North America belonged to England, Mexico belonged to Spain. The Spaniards built the *San Antonio de Valero* mission in the northeast part of Mexico called Texas.

This Spanish mission became known as the "Alamo mission" because of the grove of trees in which it was built. *Alamo* is the Spanish word for poplar.

A heavy adobe wall surrounded the chapel, hospital, convent, and yard of this mission that covered several acres. It was built like a fort in this land of hostile Indians it served. After about seventy-five

years the mission was abandoned, and parts of it crumbled into ruins.

During this time, the American colonies had won their independence from England. Then in 1821, Mexico won its freedom from Spain after a long struggle. Now the Mexican people could choose their own leaders, as the citizens of the United States could.

There were few settlers in the part of Mexico called Texas. It was a barren land of deserts and mountains. The Indians, who had become good horsemen, were fierce fighters. They did not welcome settlers on the land, and often raided the small farms.

During the year that Mexico won its independence a brilliant American lawyer moved to Texas. His name was Stephen Austin. He believed that if enough farmers settled there it could become a prosperous place. He talked to the leaders of the new Mexican government about it. He told them that Americans would be willing to live in Texas if they could farm the land. They would become citizens of Mexico, and they would be good citizens, he said. They would raise crops, build towns and schools, and make Texas a safe place to live.

The Mexicans liked the idea. They knew Americans would work hard to build good farms and towns. Nobody else wanted to try to tame the wild, barren place, so why not let the Americans try? The Mexicans offered each settler 4,000 acres of free land. Of course, much of the land was sandy, and it looked worthless for growing crops. But thousands of Americans came to Texas, and they worked hard to raise crops and cattle. They used water from the rivers for irrigation and cotton, wheat and some vegetables grew. They found hardy breeds of cattle that could feed on small amounts of grass. They built log cabins and adobe houses and schools.

In 1824 Mexico adopted a constitution that was much like the American Constitution. It guaranteed freedom to the citizens under a democratic government, similar to that of the United States. Texas was part of a larger state in Mexico, but it was promised that when there were enough people living there, it would be a separate state with its own capital and state courts. The former Americans living in Texas wanted to be good Mexican citizens. As long as their new country was a democracy and allowed them to vote for their leaders, they could live as free men.

But soon things were not going so well in Mexico. Politicians and military leaders began fighting over who was going to lead the government. They ignored the rules in the Constitution about the people voting to choose their leaders. First one leader came into power, then another.

Some of the government leaders in Mexico began to worry about the growing number of Americans in Texas. The United States government offered to buy Texas from Mexico. But the Mexicans would not sell it. Mexico passed a law forbidding any more Americans to move to Texas. Soldiers were sent to Texas, and soon there were some fights between the soldiers and the American settlers.

Shortly afterward, a strong military leader named General Antonio López de Santa Anna seized the leadership of the Mexican government. He became the country's president as well as general of the army. Santa Anna soon showed that he didn't believe in democracy. He threw out the Constitution of 1824 and said the people couldn't elect their leaders anymore.

The people of Texas sent Stephen Austin to the country's capital, Mexico City, to ask Santa Anna to allow Texas to be a separate state in Mexico. Austin reminded Santa Anna and his leaders of the promise to let Texas have its own state government. They refused to allow it. This made Austin angry, and he wrote a letter to all the people of Texas, including those of Mexican descent, asking them to help set up a state government there. When Santa Anna heard about this he had his soldiers throw Austin in jail. Austin had to stay in jail for almost two years before he was allowed to go home to Texas.

The Texans were glad to see their representative again, and they held a big banquet to celebrate his return. Up until he was imprisoned, Austin had been in favor of supporting the Mexican government. Now that he saw that people could not be free under Santa Anna's government, he said, "Our only choice is war." The Texans still believed in being part of a democratic Mexico, but they did not want to live under Santa Anna's rule. If he sent any more soldiers to make them obey him, they would fight them.

Austin had help in his leadership of the Texans from three colorful men. One of them was Sam Houston, a big, rough man who had been an Indian scout, a soldier, a U.S. Congressman, and a governor of Tennessee. He had resigned as governor of Tennessee to move west and find a more exciting life. He found this life in Texas and he liked the young, wild, growing place. People soon looked to him for leadership, for he was experienced in both politics and military matters.

Another natural leader was Jim Bowie, a famous frontier fighter whose bravery was a legend. He had grown up in the wilderness of Louisiana, but felt at home among the wealthy businessmen of New Orleans, too. He was a good businessman himself. There were many robbers who attacked travelers on lonely wilderness roads, and Jim Bowie often traveled alone. But he was such a fierce fighter that he often killed the attackers.

Bowie had a metal smith make a special knife for him, and it came to be known as the Bowie knife. It had a special shape to the blade and a hand guard for protection in knife fights. It was such a deadly weapon that not many robbers wanted to have anything to do with attacking Jim Bowie. His name became famous everywhere.

The third leader was William Travis, who was called "Buck." He was a tough, hot-tempered man, but he was also well-educated. He was a lawyer and

BOWIE KNIFE

HOUSTON

BOWIE

he had taught school before moving to Texas. He didn't like the soldiers of Santa Anna's government, and he was among the first Texans to get into fights with them. He was thrown into jail and whipped after one fight, and his fellow Texans were so enraged by this that they sent an armed force to attack a Mexican fort. They fought so well that the commander surrendered, and Buck Travis was released from jail.

Soon Travis, Bowie and Austin were leading armed groups of men against Mexican troops. They drove the Mexicans out of several Texas towns and captured some forts. They declared they would fight un-

TRAVIS

AUSTIN

til Santa Anna restored the Constitution of 1824 and made Mexico a democracy again.

The Texans decided to form their own government until the fight with Santa Anna was settled. They chose representatives, and these men met and named a governor, Henry Smith. They appointed Sam Houston Commander-in-Chief of the Regular Texas Army. Besides the Regular Army, there were groups of volunteers who fought, too.

When Santa Anna heard about his troops being defeated he was furious. "Those Texans have gone too far," he said. "Now I am going to crush them." The famous general ordered 5,000 soldiers to march to Texas, and he commanded the army himself. The Texans did not have that many troops, and Santa Anna felt sure he could kill them all or make them surrender.

While this big army was marching toward Texas, a band of 300 volunteers attacked the Mexican troops who were using the abandoned Alamo mission as a fort. The high, thick walls made of adobe running all around the mission still stood. There was a large, open courtyard inside the walls. It made a very good fort, because bullets could not go through the thick walls.

The Mexicans felt secure in this fort. But the Texas volunteers fought so hard that the Mexicans retreated and left the Alamo and the whole town of San Antonio to them.

The Alamo stood right in the path where Santa Anna's army would come as it advanced toward the biggest Texas towns. The Texans decided to use the Alamo as a fort to stop the Mexicans.

Buck Travis and Jim Bowie each arrived at the Alamo with a group of armed volunteers. They decided to combine the forces and share the command of the troops. The Regular Army was not at the Alamo, and Sam Houston was over in the eastern part of Texas talking with the Cherokee Indian leaders. The Mexicans had tried to get the Indians to fight against the Texans, but Houston talked them out of it. He had lived among the Indians and he liked them. They trusted Houston and did not fight.

On the morning of February 8, 1836, the people in San Antonio and the Alamo cheered and went on a week-long celebration to welcome a special visitor. He was none other than Davy Crockett, the most famous frontiersman in the world. He was even more famous than Jim Bowie. He had lived in the wilderness of Tennessee when he was growing up, and he had been an expert bear hunter. He had also been a scout and a soldier, fighting under Andrew Jackson against the Indians.

Davy Crockett was said to be the best rifle shot in

the world. People said he could shoot the string of a kite in half when it was flying in a high wind.

He was a big, tall man, and he wore the homemade clothes of the frontier. He sometimes wore a coonskin cap with a tail hanging in back, and buckskin trousers and Indian moccasins. Davy liked people and he loved to tell stories about his adventures in the wilderness. Wherever he went, crowds of people gathered around him to hear him tell stories. He had been a congressman from Tennessee like Sam Houston, but he, too, left that life for more adventure.

The men in the Alamo were glad to see Davy Crockett, for they knew he would be a good man to have with them in a fight. They wanted to make him a colonel in the volunteers. "No, I'll just be kind of a high private," Davy told them. He carried his famous rifle, "Old Betsy."

There were now almost two hundred men in the Alamo, and they had quite a bit of food stored inside, in case they were surrounded by Mexicans. They knew they would need help from many more men if Santa Anna's big army attacked. They hoped they could hold out until help arrived. Jim Bowie ordered a sentry to stay in the tall tower of a church in the town to watch for the Mexican army.

Finally, at dawn on the morning of February 23, 1836, the sentry spotted a huge mass of men far off

on the horizon. It was Santa Anna's army. He rang the bell with all his strength, and the Texas volunteers hurried into the Alamo. The long-awaited fight was coming.

Buck Travis had sent Jim Bonham, a famous scout and horseman, to another fort miles away to ask for help. He was sure more Texans would arrive soon. But when Bonham galloped back into the Alamo, he brought word that the commander of the other fort refused to send his troops. They were needed at the other fort, he said.

Santa Anna set up headquarters in the town of San Antonio. He sent a messenger to the Alamo, telling the Texans to surrender. They refused. Then he

sent word that he would take no prisoners when the fort was captured. Everyone inside would be killed.

The Mexicans surrounded the Alamo and dug trenches for soldiers. But when they dared to come close to the fort, Davy Crockett picked them off with deadly aim. They were amazed at his shooting ability. But even though many of their soldiers were killed, the Mexicans kept bringing big cannon closer and closer to the Alamo.

After a couple of days, Santa Anna ordered the cannon to open fire. From then on there was a constant roar, day and night, as the guns blasted the fort. The Texans held their fire to save ammunition.

They knew the Mexicans would finally try to send men over the walls. With less than two hundred men they could not fight off Santa Anna's thousands of troops forever. They would need their ammunition if the Mexicans came pouring over the walls.

In the days that followed, Santa Anna's soldiers rushed toward the Alamo again and again. But each time the Texans' deadly fire was so accurate that the attacks failed. Davy Crockett from his post at the wall sent many enemy soldiers running for safety. They had never seen such fierce fighters as these trapped Texans.

Jim Bowie had injured his leg and then caught pneumonia. Soon he had a high fever and grew weaker and weaker. After a few days he had to lie on a cot in one of the rooms, too ill to fight anymore. Buck Travis took command of the whole group of volunteers and continued to lead the defense. The Mexicans kept firing day and night, and the men in the Alamo could not take time to sleep. Every man was needed at his post on the wall, no matter how tired he was.

Buck Travis sent messages to leaders in other parts of Texas, begging for help. Time and again daring horsemen rode out of the fort at breakneck speed, dashing through the enemy lines as bullets flew around them. One of them rode to find Sam Houston, but it was such a long ride that it took days. Another rider reached a fort where some Texas volunteers were, and the commander ordered men and supplies to start toward the Alamo. But as they bumped along over the dusty land, three of the supply wagons broke down. While they were trying to fix the wagons, another messenger told the commander that a thousand Mexican troops were getting ready to attack their own fort. He decided to send his men back to defend their fort.

When big Sam Houston got word that the Alamo was surrounded and under attack, he set out with Regular Army troops to rescue it. But it was a long march, and it would take days to get there.

Meanwhile, the tired defenders of the Alamo were running lower and lower on ammunition. With every attack the troops of Santa Anna managed to get closer and closer to the walls of the fort. The men inside knew now that help would not come in time. They knew they were going to die, but they vowed to fight to the end to prevent Santa Anna from taking over Texas. They were fighting for a free, democratic government and were willing to give their lives for liberty, just as Americans had before them. Their flag, flying atop the highest wall, was the flag of Mexico with the words "Constitution of 1824" lettered in the middle. They wanted to be good citizens of a free Mexico to the end.

After many days of pounding, the Mexican cannon finally blasted a huge hole in the north wall of the old mission. Other cannon kept firing at the other walls. The defenders inside kept fighting back bravely, but it was getting more dangerous all the time.

In the meantime, a group of Texas leaders met at a convention many miles away in a town called Washington-on-the-Brazos. They decided that Texans could no longer live under the tyranny of Santa Anna, and they declared, as representatives of the people, that Texas was now independent from Mexico. They set up a Republic of Texas and chose a temporary President, David Burnet, until the war with Santa Anna was over.

On the night of March 5, the guns of Santa Anna's army fell silent. The tired defenders in the Alamo tried to get some sleep to be ready for the next attack. Santa Anna was clever. He knew they were so exhausted they would find it hard to wake up again.

The time for the final attack had come. At five o'clock the next morning thousands of Mexican troops rushed the Alamo. They flung ladders up against the walls so they could climb over. The weary Texans struggled to awaken and grab their guns.

Manning the top of the walls, they put up a fierce fight, killing as many as seven enemy soldiers for every one of them that died. But there were too many enemy troops. And more and more kept coming. One by one the brave defenders died fighting.

Twice the troops of Santa Anna were driven back, but more soldiers were sent to attack again. Finally there were so few defenders left that the Mexicans came pouring over the walls. Buck Travis died at the cannon he was firing. Then Davy Crockett fell dead, surrounded by enemy dead. The Texans fought with clubs, knives and anything else they had, but they were overwhelmed. Santa Anna's troops rushed into the room where Jim Bowie lay sick on his cot and killed him. At last there were no more defenders alive. The brave fight was over.

Sam Houston was on his way to the Alamo with his troops when a messenger gave him the news that the Alamo had fallen. Santa Anna was marching toward the towns along the Gulf of Mexico and planned to conquer all of Texas. There would be no freedom for Texas if he succeeded.

The Mexican general felt sure the Texans would be so frightened that they would surrender and give up their ideas of freedom. But when Houston and all the other people of Texas heard about the brave fight put up by the men in the Alamo, they were not frightened. They were more determined than ever to fight Santa Anna and win freedom.

In the following weeks Santa Anna marched his men across Texas, chasing after David Burnet and the other leaders of the new Texas government. Sam Houston retreated, but he kept adding men to his army and it grew bigger.

At last Houston saw his chance. Santa Anna and his troops were camped on a peninsula on the coast where they could be trapped. Houston rushed with eight hundred men, marching day and night, until he reached the spot were the enemy was. His scouts destroyed the bridge over which Santa Anna might escape. He was trapped.

It was broad daylight and the Mexican soldiers were not expecting an attack by any large group. Suddenly Sam Houston yelled to his men, "Remember the Alamo!" That was all the furious Texans needed. They attacked fiercely. Charging, shooting, and swinging swords, they overwhelmed the Mexican troops. In a short time they had completely defeated the enemy, and the Mexicans surrendered.

All except Santa Anna, that is. The wily general managed to escape on a fast horse in the confusion of the battle. He changed his uniform for some plain work clothes and tried to hide out. But he was soon discovered and brought back to Sam Houston as a

prisoner. Houston had been shot in the ankle and he lay propped up against a tree when Santa Anna was brought to him. With bitter memories of the men killed at the Alamo, he could have ordered the enemy general shot. But Houston was not as cruel as Santa Anna, and he decided to let the general live and go back to Mexico.

First, though, Santa Anna had to agree to sign a treaty recognizing Texas as a free and independent republic. He also had to agree to remove his army from Texas and not come back again. Santa Anna signed quickly and was glad to escape alive after all the cruel things he had done.

There was great celebrating all over Texas, for at last the people were free to live under a democratic government. Sam Houston was a hero, and the people elected him President of the Republic of Texas. They also voted to ratify a constitution that guaranteed freedom.

After a while things got better for the Mexican people, too. The Constitution of 1824 was restored and the people had a democratic government again. Mexico has been a democracy ever since.

Texas remained an independent country until 1845. Then the people voted to join the United States and it became the state of Texas. Texans and other Americans have always remembered the Alamo and the brave men who died there. They fought so that others might have freedom, and the battle of the Alamo will always be a shining chapter in history.

About the Author: Norman Richards grew up in a small New England town. A descendant of early colonial settlers, he developed a love of history as a child. He holds a journalism degree from Boston University and has traveled over much of the world in his career as a writer and magazine editor. He is the author of fifteen books for young readers and more than one hundred magazine articles. Mr. Richards lives with his wife and three children in the wooded countryside of Connecticut, not far from New York City.

About the Illustrator: Tom Dunnington grew up in Iowa and Minnesota. He began his art training in Indiana and continued it at the Art Institute and the American Academy of Art in Chicago. Mr. Dunnington works almost full time as a free-lance artist. He teaches one class in illustration at the Layton School of Art in Milwaukee, Wisconsin. He has five children and lives in Elmhurst, west of Chicago.